101

QUESTIONS & ANSWERS

The World of Dinosaurs

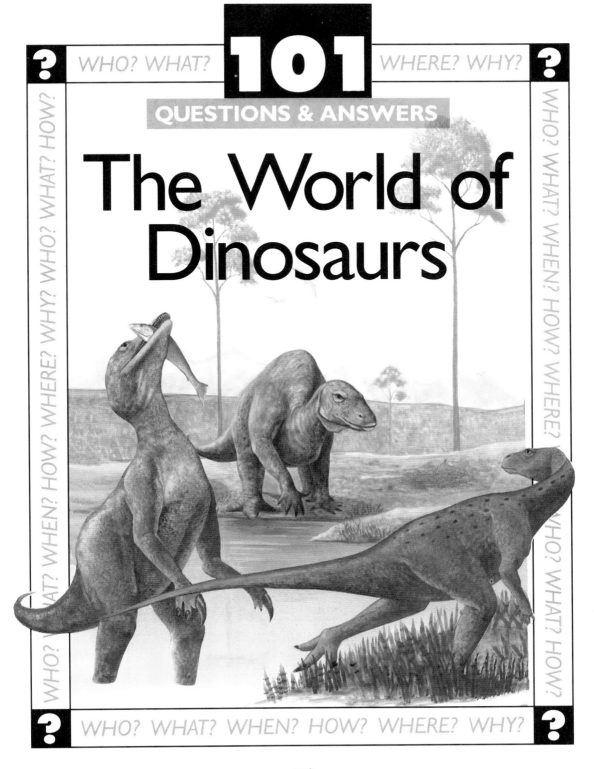

Facts On File®

AN INFOBASE HOLDINGS COMPANY

GLOSSARY

ammonites A group of animals related to squid, but with coiled external shells. They died out 65 million years ago.

beak A horny covering of the jaw bone found in birds and some dinosaurs.

belemnites Squid-like animals with hard shells inside. They died out 65 million years ago.

browsing Feeding by picking leaves, shoots and bark from trees and shrubs.

cannibalism Feeding on your own kind.

climate The overall weather conditions of temperature, rainfall and weather in a certain part of the world.

climatic Relating to climate.

continents The major areas of land on the Earth's surface. Modern continents include Africa, Asia and Australia.

crest A raised area on the head, in many animals used for display.

evolve Change over a long period of time and many generations.

extinct Completely died out.

fossil Remains or traces in rocks of animals and plants that once lived.

fossilize Turn into a fossil.

gizzard The second part of a bird's stomach, used for grinding food and often containing grit. At least some dinosaurs are thought to have had a similar gizzard.

heat-exchanger A structure for transferring heat between two mediums.

hoof A tough horny toenail on which an animal stands.

horn A hard tough material made of the same chemical as hair. It forms a protective layer on the outside of parts of some animals. The pointed horns of cows are covered in horn, and similar pointed structures on heads are also called horns.

impression A mark left where something was against, or contained in, a rock.

lemurs Mammals related to monkeys, but with more primitive characteristics.

mammal A furred, warm-blooded backboned animal that produces live young and feeds them on milk.

meteorite A piece of rock from space that crashes to Earth.

missing link An unknown animal, linking two known types in evolution. Often applied (wrongly) to known links such as Archaeopteryx.

paleontologist Scientist who studies fossils and ancient life.

plaster of Paris A mixture of water and fine plaster powder that sets hard when it dries. It can be used to make casts and protective coverings.

prey An animal that is hunted and eaten by another.

reptile A cold-blooded backboned animal with scales that lays eggs on land.

restoration A lifelike picture or model of an extinct animal.

rodent A mammal with gnawing teeth, such as a mouse, squirrel or porcupine.

scales Small horny, plate-like pieces of skin that form the outer covering of most reptiles and fish.

scavenger An animal that feeds on dead animals that it has not killed itself.

species A kind of animal or plant — all those living things that look alike and can breed with one another.

spinal cord The main bundle of nerves that runs down the backbone of an animal.

The 101 Questions and Answers series contains six titles that cover a range of scientific topics popular with young readers, such as: the human body, geology, basic mechanics and physics, dinosaurs, and transportation. Each book is designed in a question-and-answer format with color illustrations throughout.

The World of Dinosaurs

Library of Congress Cataloging-in-Publication Data
Stidworthy, John, 1943-
        The World of Dinosaurs / [John Stidworthy]
        p.   cm. -- (101 questions & answers)
        Includes index.
        ISBN 0-8160-3215-7
        1. Dinosaurs--Miscellanea--Juvenile literature.   [1. dinosaurs--Miscellanea.   2. Questions and answers.]   I. Title.   II. Series.
        QE862.D5S723   1995
        567.9'1--dc20   95-16305

Acknowledgments
Designer: Ben White
Project Editor: Lionel Bender
Text Editor: Madeleine Samuel
Media Conversion and Typesetting: Peter MacDonald and Una Macnamara
Managing Editor: David Riley
Production Controller: Ruth Charlton

All artwork by Martin Knowelden except 4tr, 27b, 28t, 30t by Ann Winterbotham; 10t, 15l, 17tr, 25c by Hayward Art Group; 9b, 34t by Brian McIntyre; 28b by Peter Bull Art Studio; and 32-33t by John Butler/Ian Fleming Associates.
(t = top, b = bottom, l = left, r = right).

CONTENTS

This book contains questions and answers on the following topics:

John Stidworthy

Who first found dinosaurs?

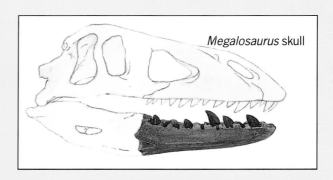

Megalosaurus skull

Dinosaur bones were probably first found hundreds of years ago but at the time they were thought to be parts of giants. The first remains recognized as those of huge reptiles were fossil teeth found in 1822 by Mary Mantell in Sussex, England.

◁ Mary Mantell and Gideon's *Iguanodon* drawing.

Dr. Gideon Mantell, Mary's husband, studied the bones and discovered they were like those of the iguana lizard, but much bigger. In 1825 he called the big reptile *Iguanodon*. The first dinosaur named was *Megalosaurus* in 1824, but the word *dinosaur*, meaning "terrible lizard," wasn't invented until 1841.

▽ Since 1822 whole skeletons of *Iguanodon* have been found. Now we know that the "horn" in Mantell's drawing is the spiky thumb bone.

Iguanodon 30 ft (9 m) long

Who fought the Bone Wars?

These desperadoes were dinosaur bone hunters in the United States. They needed guns to fend off hostile Indians and rival bone collectors. On the right in the back row is Othniel Marsh. In the 1870s and '80s he and another fossil hunter, Edward Cope, competed to become champion dinosaur finder of America. At times their men came to blows. Marsh and Cope found 136 new kinds of dinosaurs.

Can I find a dinosaur?

Yes, since dinosaur bones are still being found in many parts of the world. Some are collected on expeditions by specialists, but amateur collectors can make exciting finds. In 1983, a Mr. Bill Walker discovered a new dinosaur, now called *Baryonyx walkeri* after him, in southern England.

New discovery of dinos
A claw, a finger and a humerus bone from an
____ and ____ been named *Baryonyx walkeri*, ____

◁ Bill Walker holds the 12 in- (31 cm) long claw of the meat-eating dinosaur he found.

△ We still do not know how *Baryonyx* used its claws or which feet they were on.

Where are fossils found?

Dinosaur fossils are scattered in rocks that formed from mud or sand laid down between 225 million and 65 million years ago. Where these rocks are accessible, we may find fossils and dig them out.

The map shows the most important places where dinosaur fossils have been found. Western North America, East Africa, the Gobi Desert and parts of China are some of the best places for dinosaur hunters.

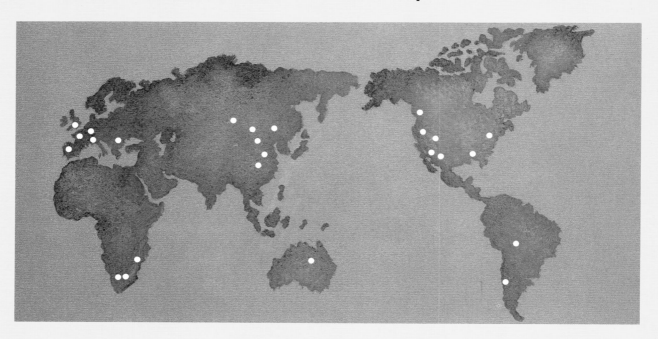

How are fossils dug up?

A dinosaur's bones are chipped out from rock using chisels. Loose rock is brushed away. When the bones are ready to be carried to a museum, they are wrapped in bandages soaked in plaster of Paris, or enclosed in a jacket of polyurethane foam. This makes a shell that protects them from damage on their journey.

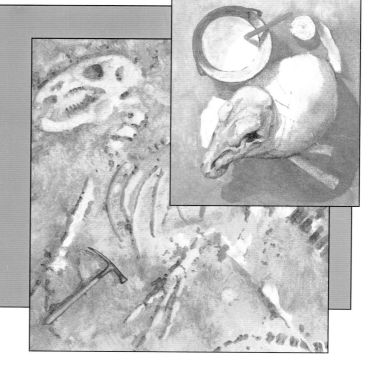

Can we rebuild their skeletons?

Yes. Museums wire individual dinosaur bones together and mount the whole skeleton on a metal frame for display.

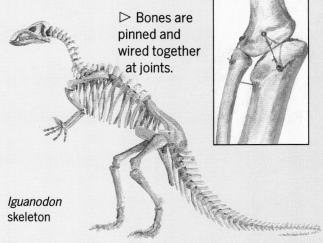

▷ Bones are pinned and wired together at joints.

Iguanodon skeleton

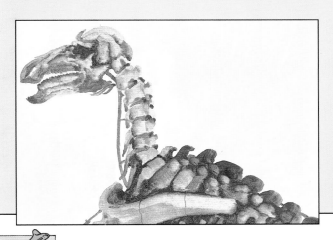

For missing parts false bones of plaster or plastic are made up. From the shape and size of the bones, and from marks and projections on them where muscles were attached, scientists can tell which bones belong where and how the dinosaur stood.

Did dinosaurs have scaly skin?

dinosaur skin impression

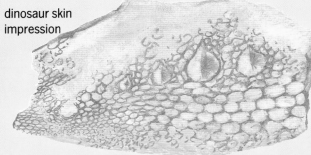

Nobody can say for sure whether some dinosaurs had soft skin, how the skin was colored, or how a dinosaur sounded or smelled.

a restoration of *Iguanodon*

Most dinosaur remains are just bones. Soft parts of dead animals rot away quickly and rarely fossilize, but some skin impressions are preserved. Dinosaurs whose skin has been found had scales or bony plates and knobs.

Skin colors are not preserved in fossils. In paintings of prehistoric animals artists have made up the colors. We think dinosaurs were colored for hiding or for signaling, like animals today, but perhaps we have got their colors all wrong.

Why are there no dinosaurs now?

Dinosaurs were one of the most successful types of animal ever to have lived. But they died out in just a few million years. By 65 million years ago they were extinct. At about this time the climate became much cooler and plant-life changed. For animals adapted to warm conditions, like dinosaurs, life became difficult. Some scientists think a sudden climatic change killed them off. This could have happened when a giant meteorite hit the Earth and threw up dust, blocking out sunlight.

△ A dust cloud from a meteorite strike could have cooled the Earth's surface.

▽ *Triceratops*, a plant-eater, may have been unable to survive the cold.

DID YOU KNOW...
● Many other animals, including pterodactyls and ammonites, died out 65 million years ago?
● Iridium, a metal common in meteorites but rare on Earth, is mostly found in rocks 65 million years old?

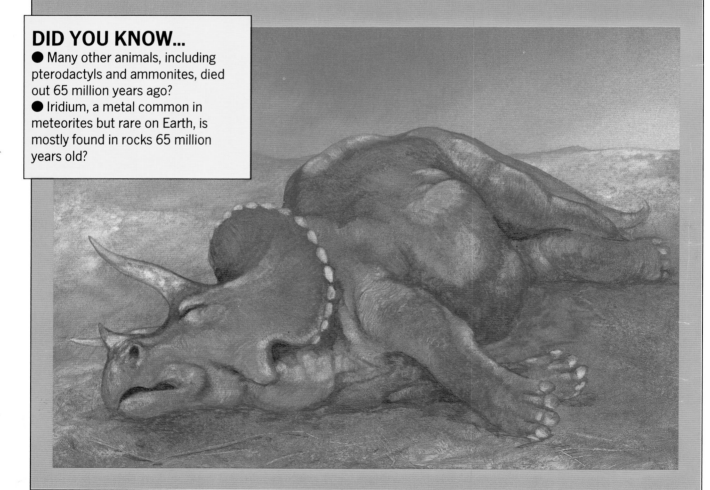

What replaced dinosaurs?

Plesiadapis, an early relative of lemurs, lived 55 million years ago.

There were mammals around before the first dinosaurs, but as dinosaurs came to rule the mammals did not evolve or multiply greatly. Most fed on small animals such as insects. As the dinosaurs declined, the mammals grew in number. Perhaps their furry bodies better suited a cooler climate? Once the dinosaurs died out, the mammals took over.

Changes in numbers toward the end of the Age of Dinosaurs

Within a few million years, large mammals arose, including many plant-eaters. Some evolved into early types of elephants, camels and horses. They took over the ways of life of the big dinosaurs.

1 *Aepycamelus*, a primitive camel
2 *Amebelodon*, an early elephant
3 *Pliohippus*, ancestor of the horse
4 *Epigaulus*, an early rodent

What was *Archaeopteryx*?

The fossil *Archaeopteryx* is well known as a "missing link" between reptiles and birds. It had feathers like a bird but its skeleton was similar to that of a small, running meat-eating dinosaur such as *Compsognathus*.

Archaeopteryx

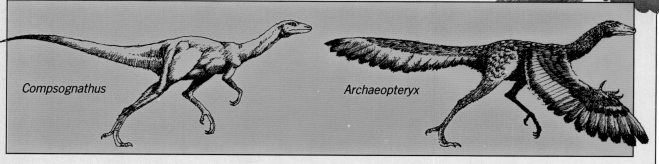

Compsognathus

Archaeopteryx

Did dinosaurs have feathers?

We cannot be sure, but several small dinosaurs may have had. Feathers are more finely divided than typical reptile scales but like them are made of horny material grown in the skin. Some scientists think a ridge on the arm bones of dinosaurs like *Avimimus* supported feathers. However, the animal's arms were too short for flying.

Avimimus

How did birds start to fly?

Archaeopteryx was the size of a magpie.

Archaeopteryx had feathers on its wings and tail. It could certainly glide and may have been able to fly by flapping its wings. Perhaps the first birds climbed trees, as shown here and glided between them. But it is more likely they began to fly by holding wings out as they were running.

Only five skeletons of *Archaeopteryx* have ever been found. Two of the specimens were kept in museums for many years before they were identified as *Archaeopteryx*.

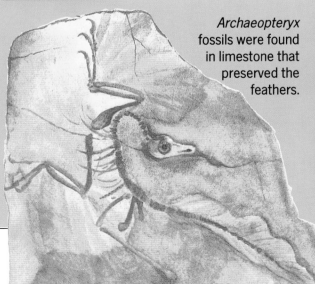

Archaeopteryx fossils were found in limestone that preserved the feathers.

WAS IT REALLY A BIRD?

Feathers and a special shoulder bone, the wishbone, are the hallmarks of a bird. *Archaeopteryx* had feathers; their impressions are clear in fossils like this one. Their microscopic structure is like that of bird feathers today. *Archaeopteryx* also had a wishbone. But like a reptile, it had small teeth and a long bony tail.

Which was the biggest dinosaur?

The largest dinosaurs belonged to a group called the sauropods, meaning "reptile feet." These included well-known kinds such as *Diplodocus* and *Apatosaurus*. But for sheer bulk these were dwarfed by *Brachiosaurus*. Like other sauropods, this animal had a long neck and long tail and walked on all fours. But, unlike most, its front legs were longer than its hind legs. Its shoulders were higher than its hips, and its head could reach 43 ft (13 m) from the ground. *Brachiosaurus* is the biggest dinosaur for which we have a nearly whole skeleton, but in 1972 and 1979 bones of even larger animals were discovered. These dinosaurs are named *Supersaurus* and *Ultrasaurus*.

—— Ultrasaurus
—— Supersaurus
—— Brachiosaurus

Key

Coelophysis			
Compsognathus			
Ornithomimus			
Deinonychus			
Saurornithoides			
Archaeopteryx			
Megalosaurus			
Allosaurus			
Ceratosaurus			
Tyrannosaurus			
Plateosaurus			
Melanorosaurus			
Cetiosaurus			
Brachiosaurus			
Diplodocus			
Alamosaurus			
Heterodontosaurus			
Camptosaurus			
Iguanodon			
Trachodon			
Parasaurolophus			
Protoceratops			
Triceratops			
Pachycephalosaurus			
Stegosaurus			
Dravidosaurus			
Hylaeosaurus			
Ankylosaurus			

HOW BIG IS BIG?

Brachiosaurus was 74 ft (22.5 m) long. Its weight is calculated at 84.5 tons. If *Supersaurus* was in proportion to the few bones that have been found, it may have been 54.5 ft (16.5 m) tall and 99 ft (30 m) long. *Ultrasaurus* bones could have weighed 143 tons.

▽ Dinosaurs from many different groups are shown to scale. Many were huge animals by today's standards, but there were also some the size of a person or smaller.

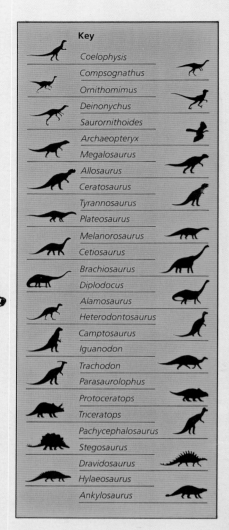

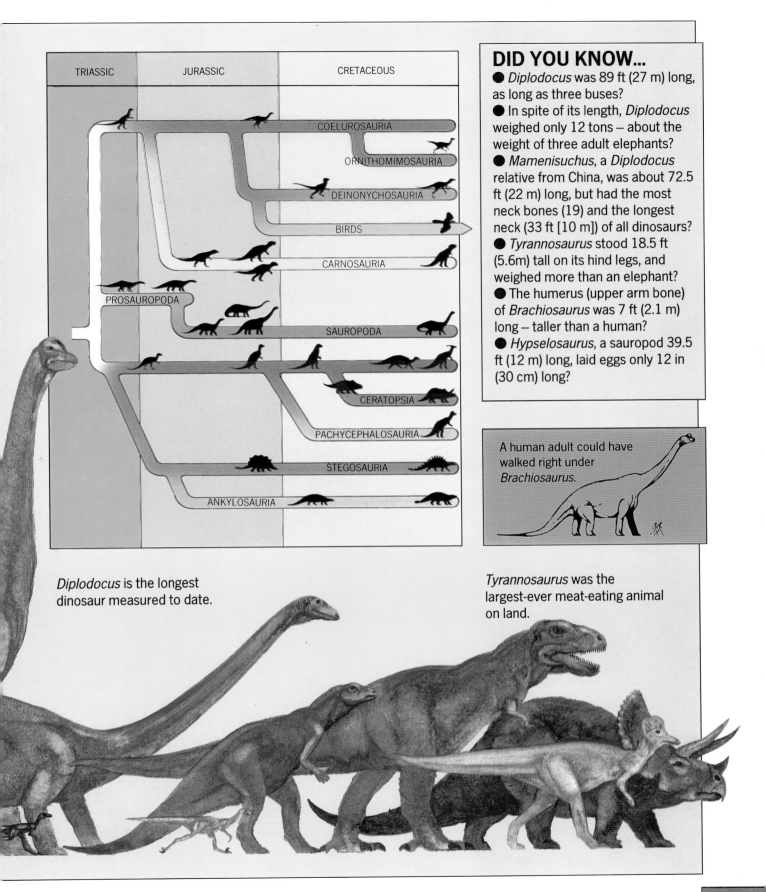

TRIASSIC	JURASSIC	CRETACEOUS

COELUROSAURIA

ORNITHOMIMOSAURIA

DEINONYCHOSAURIA

BIRDS

CARNOSAURIA

PROSAUROPODA

SAUROPODA

CERATOPSIA

PACHYCEPHALOSAURIA

STEGOSAURIA

ANKYLOSAURIA

DID YOU KNOW...

● *Diplodocus* was 89 ft (27 m) long, as long as three buses?

● In spite of its length, *Diplodocus* weighed only 12 tons — about the weight of three adult elephants?

● *Mamenisuchus*, a *Diplodocus* relative from China, was about 72.5 ft (22 m) long, but had the most neck bones (19) and the longest neck (33 ft [10 m]) of all dinosaurs?

● *Tyrannosaurus* stood 18.5 ft (5.6m) tall on its hind legs, and weighed more than an elephant?

● The humerus (upper arm bone) of *Brachiosaurus* was 7 ft (2.1 m) long — taller than a human?

● *Hypselosaurus*, a sauropod 39.5 ft (12 m) long, laid eggs only 12 in (30 cm) long?

A human adult could have walked right under *Brachiosaurus*.

Diplodocus is the longest dinosaur measured to date.

Tyrannosaurus was the largest-ever meat-eating animal on land.

13

Which were the first dinosaurs?

The first animals we can recognize as dinosaurs lived about 225 million years ago. To begin with, dinosaurs were small animals about 3 ft (1 m) long, running on their hind legs. *Procompsognathus* was one of them. It ate smaller animals. *Plateosaurus* was one of the first large dinosaurs. It grew to 20 ft (6 m) long and fed on plants.

Euparkeria

Dinosaurs evolved from thecodonts ("socket-teeth") like *Euparkeria* and *Ornithosuchus*. They walked on four legs.

DID YOU KNOW...
● Crocodiles had the same ancestors as dinosaurs and so are the closest living relatives of birds?

Ornithosuchus

Plateosaurus 1
Procompsognathus 2
Kuhneosaurus, a gliding lizard 3
Protosuchus, an early crocodile, lived on land 4
Early mammal 5

Why were they so successful?

Early dinosaurs were among the first animals to evolve legs tucked right underneath the body. This is the best place for supporting great weight or moving fast to catch prey or escape enemies. It may well have given them an advantage over other animals around.

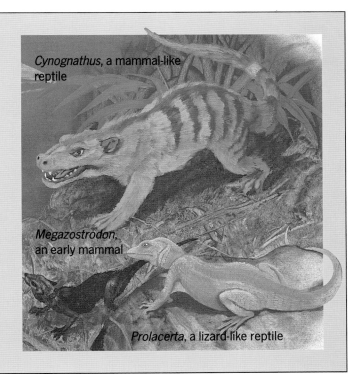

Cynognathus, a mammal-like reptile

Megazostrodon, an early mammal

Prolacerta, a lizard-like reptile

What were their teeth like?

Dinosaurs had different teeth according to what they ate. But most had a mouth full of similar teeth. Exceptions were *Heterodontosaurus* and its relations. They were plant-eaters and only about 4 ft (1.2 m) long. They had three different types of teeth just as we do: sharp pointed teeth in the front, fang-like ones at the side, and grinders at the back.

Heterodontosaurus

This dinosaur could chew from side to side like a cow.

Heterodontosaurus skull

Which were the smallest?

Over 100 years ago, in southern Germany, an almost perfect specimen was found of an adult meat-eating dinosaur. The unusual thing about it was its size – only 28 in (70 cm) long overall, most of which was tail. This chicken-sized animal, called *Compsognathus*, is the smallest adult dinosaur known. Few specimens have been found, but one from France is nearly twice as long. Perhaps dinosaurs, like crocodiles, carried on growing even after they were adult and able to breed?

◁ *Ornitholestes* had three long fingers with claws for grasping prey like lizards.

▽ Three *Compsognathus* chase insects beside their larger relative *Ornitholestes*

Compso-gnathus 1
Ornitholestes 2

Small as a mouse?

Mussasaurus ("mouse-lizard") skeletons were discovered in Argentina. Each would fit into the palm of your hand. Eggs 1 in (2.5 cm) long were found nearby, so the tiny skeletons must have been babies. Adult *Mussasaurus* may have been about 10 ft (3 m) long, but they probably looked like *Plateosaurus* (see page 14).

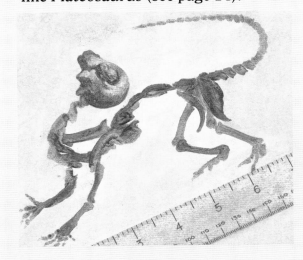

Were most dinosaurs big?

Perhaps not. It is rare for an animal to become fossilized after death. The bodies of small animals are much more likely to be eaten and their delicate bones broken into pieces. Perhaps there were many kinds of small dinosaur similar to *Compsognathus* but they left no traces.

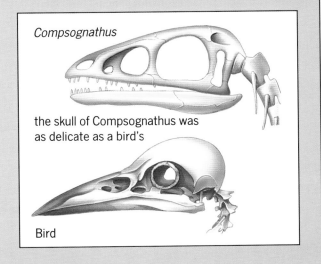

Compsognathus

the skull of Compsognathus was as delicate as a bird's

Bird

What did small dinosaurs eat?

Worms, insects, small mammals and reptiles were available. *Compsognathus* could run fast and catch quick moving prey. The first *Compsognathus* skeleton found had the remains of a lizard inside it, its last meal!

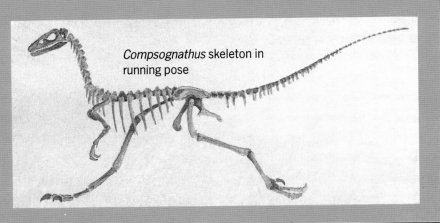

Compsognathus skeleton in running pose

Which was the fastest runner?

Struthiomimus lived toward the end of the Age of Dinosaurs. It was shaped like an ostrich, except for the long tail. Its legs were long and thin but had three toes rather than two. *Struthiomimus* could have run at 30 miles (50 km) an hour – as fast as an ostrich or horse. It used its speed mainly to escape big meat-eaters like *Tyrannosaurus*. *Struthiomimus* had no teeth, just a horny beak. Probably, like an ostrich, it ate leaves, seeds, berries and small animals.

Toothless *Struthiomimus* is sometimes portrayed as an egg-eater.

Did it climb or did it run?

Hypsilophodon lived about 115 million years ago. Because it was lightly built and had long toes, it was thought to have been good at climbing trees. But a closer look at its skeleton has shown it was built for running. It was a plant-eater, with a horny beak to nip off leaves, and strong cheek teeth for chewing. It had big eyes and probably good sight. It may have lived like the antelopes of today.

Struthiomimus 13 ft (4 m) long

◁ The lightly built *Struthiomimus* may have used its speed to catch insects and other small animals.

▽ *Struthiomimus* running. It could swing its legs fast and take long strides like an ostrich.

▷ Each foot of *Hypsil-ophodon* had four toes. Studies of the toe bones show it could not curl its feet around branches.

Hypsilophodon 4.6–7.6 ft (1.4–2.3 m) long

DID DINOSAURS HAVE HOOFS?

Most fast-running animals stand on their toes. Some, such as deer and horses, stand on their toenails – their hoofs. Running dinosaurs, too, stood on their toes and not on the soles of their feet. As in *Hypsilophodon*, the foot and lower part of each leg were long, but the upper part was short, muscular and stocky. The part of the leg that needed to swing farthest was lightweight. On the end of its toes, it had broad hoof-like claws.

What did the fiercest dinosaurs eat?

Huge meat-eating dinosaurs, such as *Allosaurus* and *Ceratosaurus*, were especially common from 150 to 130 million years ago. This was the time when the really big plant-eaters like *Brachiosaurus* and *Diplodocus* were abundant. This suggests that these were the food of the giant meat-eaters. But some people argue that *Allosaurus* and its kind would have been too slow and weak to overpower the giant plant-eaters, and were scavengers, feeding on dinosaurs already dead.

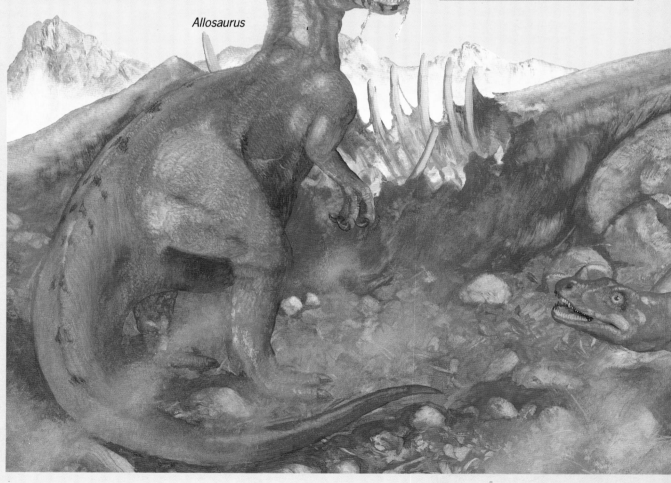

Allosaurus

WHAT WAS SPECIAL ABOUT THE MEAT-EATERS?

● Meat-eating dinosaurs had strong jaws and large numbers of big, backward-curving teeth.
● The teeth were often saw-edged, back and front, to help slice through flesh.
● Meat-eaters' skulls were large but had big gaps between some bones to make them lightweight and allow space for the biting muscles to work.
● The meat-eaters always walked on two legs.
● Their front legs had sharp claws for grasping prey.

Which was the biggest killer ever?

Tyrannosaurus rex, at 18.5 ft (5.6 m) tall, was the biggest meat-eater ever to walk the land. It could open its mouth very wide, helped by a lower jaw that bent in the middle, and use its steak-knife teeth on its prey. It lived about 70 million years ago.

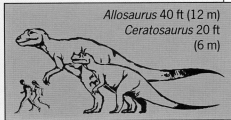

Allosaurus 40 ft (12 m)
Ceratosaurus 20 ft (6 m)

Tyrannosaurus 46 ft (14 m)

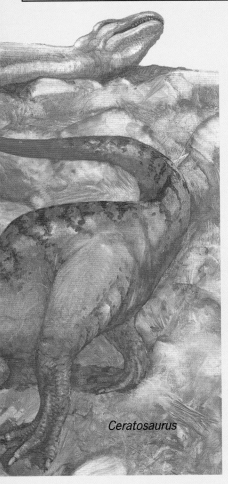

Ceratosaurus

What were the last dinosaurs like?

During the millions of years that dinosaurs ruled the world there were huge changes, for example in the kinds of plants that grew. By 70 million years ago there were flowering plants similar to those of today. Dinosaurs, too, had changed. The lumbering giants had mostly given way to smaller types, such as the duckbills like *Parasaurolophus* and horned dinosaurs like *Triceratops*. These had better jaws and teeth for dealing with the plants. Some small meat-eaters, like *Stenonychosaurus*, had a very large brain and large forward-facing eyes for hunting. They may have hunted at night, catching small mammals. Ostrich dinosaurs were common, too.

▷ Birds and mammals were present in the landscape of 70 million years ago, as well as advanced dinosaurs. Flowering plants grew alongside pines, ferns and other more primitive plants.

WHICH WAS THE BRAINIEST?
● *Stenonychosaurus* had the biggest brain for its body size of all dinosaurs, and may have been the most intelligent. About 6.5 ft (2 m) long, it would have stood waist high to a human. The large brain processed information from well-developed eyes and ears. It was a formidable hunter.

1. *Parasaurolophus*
2. *Corythosaurus*
3. *Tyrannosaurus*
4. *Triceratops*
5. *Stenonychosaurus*
6. *Struthiomimus*
7. birds
8. mammal

Changing positions
of the continents

(1) 200 million years ago

(2) 100 million years ago

(3) 1 million
years ago

CHANGING WORLD
When dinosaurs first evolved,
over 200 million years ago,
the world's continents were
joined in one landmass (1).
Each type of dinosaur could
spread throughout the world.
By 100 million years ago the
continents had begun to split
up and move apart (2) to
their present positions (3).
Different continents held
different dinosaurs

How do we know what dinosaurs ate?

An animal's jaws and teeth can tell us what it ate. Meat-eating dinosaurs mostly had dagger-shaped teeth to seize their prey. They probably tore off chunks of meat and swallowed them, rather than chewing. The plant-eaters often had teeth that chopped or crushed their food.

▷ *Plateosaurus* lived 200 million years ago.

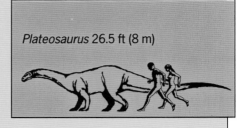

Plateosaurus 26.5 ft (8 m)

Some dinosaurs had (like birds) a gizzard between mouth and stomach. This bag had muscular walls and contained stones, which ground up plant food.

WHAT DO WE KNOW ABOUT
Plateosaurus?
● It had leaf-shaped teeth like the living iguana lizards that eat plants.
● It was one of the first plant-eating dinosaurs.
● It was one of the first plant-eaters able to walk on the ground and reach the tops of tall plants.
● It had unusual front feet; the toes could be bent back – for walking on the ground – or could be folded forward to grasp objects – perhaps to pull food to the mouth. The first finger had a large claw, which may have been used in defense.
● It may have lived in herds. Fossils have been found in groups.
● It probably ground food using its gizzard.

What reached the highest leaves?

Brachiosaurus was a huge reptile equivalent of a giraffe, built for browsing on the uppermost leaves of trees up to 43 ft (13 m) high. At the front of the mouth it had large chisel-shaped teeth, and in fossils these show signs of heavy wear. This suggests that *Brachiosaurus* fed on tough vegetation, raking it in with the teeth and grinding it in its gizzard.

Some scientists think that other big plant-eating dinosaurs, like *Diplodocus*, could also reach high into trees, by standing on their hind legs.

Brachiosaurus's powerful heart pumped blood 26.5 ft (8 m) upward to reach its head.

crest

WHAT KIND OF NOSE?
Brachiosaurus had its nostrils very high on its skull. Mammals such as tapirs and elephants are built like this. They have trunks for browsing. Maybe some dinosaurs had trunks too.

Brachiosaurus skull

DID YOU KNOW...
● *Dilophosaurus* is the earliest known large meat-eating dinosaur? It had two thin bony crests above the skull. These may have been colored and used for signaling to other dinosaurs.

Dilophosaurus skull

Which dinosaur had a sail, and why?

Ouranosaurus lived about 110 million years ago in West Africa. Even at that time, conditions there seem to have been hot and dry. This dinosaur had big spines on its backbone above the body and tail. They supported skin with many blood vessels. This "sail" was probably a heat-exchanger, allowing *Ouranosaurus* to absorb heat from the sun in the early morning or to lose extra heat in the middle of the day.

Ouranosaurus
23 ft (7 m) long

Armor or radiators?

Stegosaurus is famous as the armor-plated dinosaur. On its back it carried big diamond-shaped bony plates. For a long time they were assumed to be protection for this plant-eater against attack from meat-eating dinosaurs. But these plates were covered with skin and blood vessels, and honeycombed inside with spaces. Perhaps they helped the animal warm in the sun or keep cool? Tested in a wind tunnel, similar plates lose heat fast in a light breeze.

UP OR DOWN?

down

up

DID YOU KNOW...

● *Stegosaurus* lived in North America 145 million years ago?

● It probably had the smallest brain of any dinosaur. In a 2-ton body the brain weighed only 2.84 oz (80 g)?

● A swelling of the spinal cord (the bundle of nerves that runs inside the backbone) in the hip region of *Stegosaurus* was 20 times the size of the brain, giving rise to the idea that dinosaurs had a second brain in the tail. Actually it just marks the spot where all the nerves from the hind legs and tail joined the spinal cord.

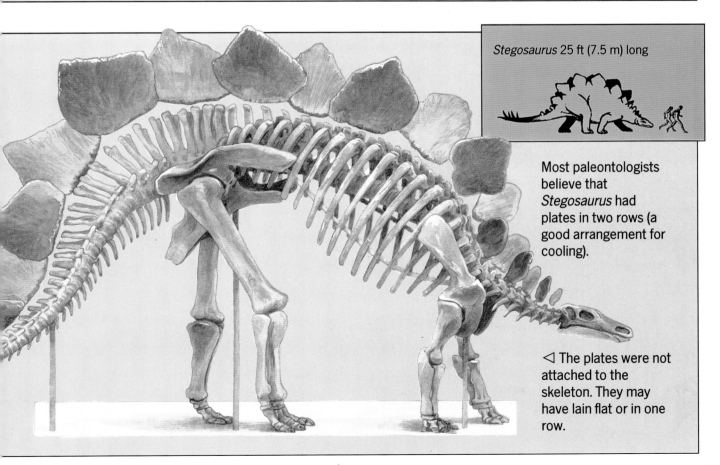

Stegosaurus 25 ft (7.5 m) long

Most paleontologists believe that *Stegosaurus* had plates in two rows (a good arrangement for cooling).

◁ The plates were not attached to the skeleton. They may have lain flat or in one row.

Pterosaur, bird or reptile?

Pterosaurs were flying reptiles only distantly related to dinosaurs. The first ones lived 220 million years ago. The last ones died out at the same time as the dinosaurs. They had features in common with both birds and bats. Pterosaurs are divided into the more primitive rhamphorhynchoids, which had long tails, and the pterodactyls, with tiny tails. Pterosaur wings were made of tough skin (not feathers) supported by the very long fourth finger of the hand.

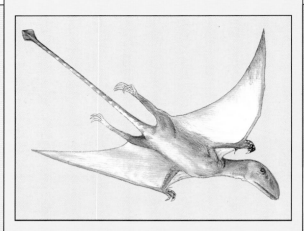

WAS IT A RUDDER?

Fossils show that the tail of the long-tailed pterosaurs like *Dimorphodon* (above) had a small flattened vane at the tip. It is usually assumed that this acted as a rudder, with the vane vertical. But when a model of such a pterosaur was made and flown, it always crashed unless the tail vane was set horizontally, acting as a flight elevator.

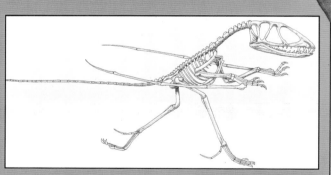

COULD THEY PERCH?

Some pterosaurs may have run on two legs, as pictured above, but generally their toes and claws look as though they would be better suited to climbing and grasping. They probably perched on trees and cliffs.

DID YOU KNOW...

● Pterosaurs could not fold their wing finger, so even if they folded their arms, their pointed wings stuck out?
● Pterosaur brains were quite large compared to most reptiles? As in birds, the part dealing with the eyes was big and their vision was good.

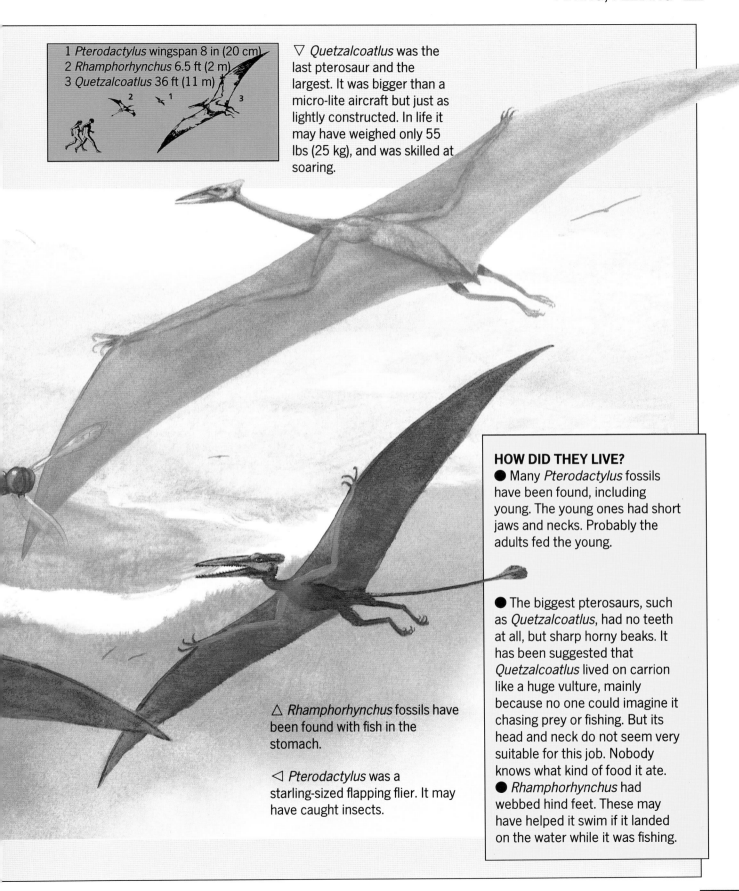

1 *Pterodactylus* wingspan 8 in (20 cm)
2 *Rhamphorhynchus* 6.5 ft (2 m)
3 *Quetzalcoatlus* 36 ft (11 m)

▽ *Quetzalcoatlus* was the last pterosaur and the largest. It was bigger than a micro-lite aircraft but just as lightly constructed. In life it may have weighed only 55 lbs (25 kg), and was skilled at soaring.

△ *Rhamphorhynchus* fossils have been found with fish in the stomach.

◁ *Pterodactylus* was a starling-sized flapping flier. It may have caught insects.

HOW DID THEY LIVE?

● Many *Pterodactylus* fossils have been found, including young. The young ones had short jaws and necks. Probably the adults fed the young.

● The biggest pterosaurs, such as *Quetzalcoatlus*, had no teeth at all, but sharp horny beaks. It has been suggested that *Quetzalcoatlus* lived on carrion like a huge vulture, mainly because no one could imagine it chasing prey or fishing. But its head and neck do not seem very suitable for this job. Nobody knows what kind of food it ate.

● *Rhamphorhynchus* had webbed hind feet. These may have helped it swim if it landed on the water while it was fishing.

Could dinosaurs swim?

Many dinosaurs may have been able to swim or wade, just like mammals such as tigers and elephants today. But dinosaurs were mainly land animals. While they ruled the land, two other groups of reptile took to the sea and became good swimmers. These were the fish-shaped, tail-propelled ichthyosaurs and the barrel-shaped plesiosaurs.

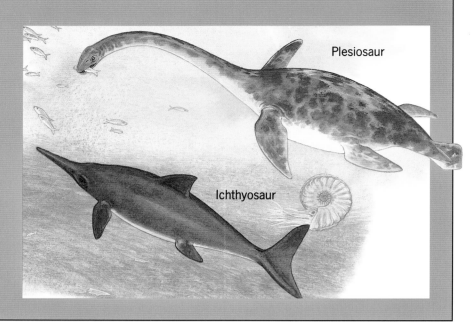

Plesiosaur

Ichthyosaur

Did ichthyo-saurs eat fish?

Ichthyosaurs swam fast by swinging their tail fins from side to side. Their backbones (below) extended into the lower parts of their tail fins. They had long narrow jaws – good for snapping – and many sharp teeth as do most fish-eaters. Fossil stomach contents show they ate fish, squid-like belemnites and ammonites.

Ichthyosaurus up to 16.5 ft (5 m) long

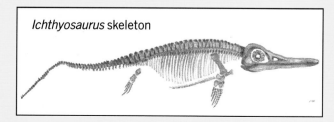

Ichthyosaurus skeleton

What lives in Loch Ness?

Some eyewitness descriptions of the Loch Ness monster describe a plesiosaur, but it is very doubtful that any survive 65 million years after the last known fossil.

Plesiosaurs had all four legs turned into paddles, with which they rowed through the water. Like ichthyosaurs, they were fish-eaters and had to surface for air.

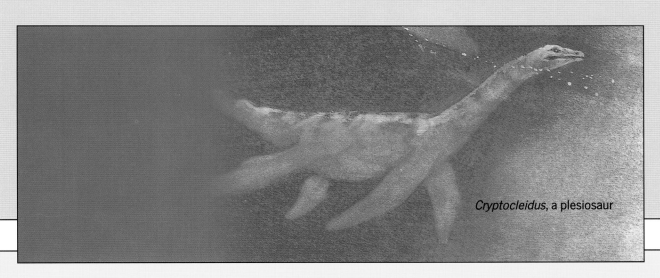

Cryptocleidus, a plesiosaur

Ichthyosaurus

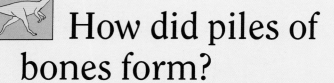

How did piles of bones form?

A few kinds of dinosaur are known from mass graves where there are many skeletons buried together. Their remains may have washed down to the same spot after they died, perhaps over a long period of time. Others lived, and died, as a group.

HERD ANIMALS?

Horned dinosaurs such as *Triceratops*, plant-eaters like *Iguanodon*, and some of the giant sauropods are among those thought to have roamed in herds.

Coelophysis 10 ft (3 m)

Can fossil footprints tell a story?

Sometimes a whole herd of dinosaurs, with adults and young, walked across mud and left prints that fossilized. From the spacing of prints we can tell if the animals were walking or running. The prints below show where a herd of *Muttaburrasaurus* were attacked by a meat-eater.

meat-eater

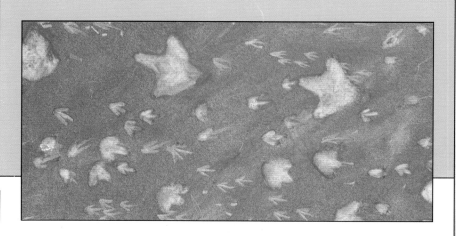

Dozens of *Coelophysis* skeletons were uncovered in one place. The animals were probably living together, but perhaps not as one happy family. Some adults had young ones inside that they had eaten!

a mass grave of *Coelophysis* in New Mexico

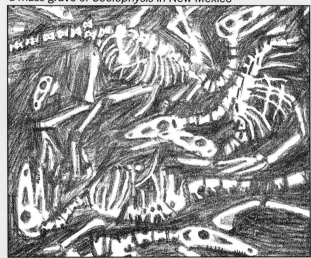

Muttaburrasaurus herd

other small dinosaurs

Did dinosaurs lay eggs?

Yes, as far as we know, all dinosaurs laid eggs, rather than giving birth to live young. Their eggs are known from several parts of the world. *Maiasaura*, a duckbill dinosaur, laid its eggs on earth mounds 10 ft (3 m) across. Nests have been found with large babies as well as eggshells. The parents looked after the babies in the nest for some time.

model of a duckbilled dinosaur's nest and eggs

Maiasaura with hatchlings

Did dinosaurs have a nesting season?

Nests of the small horned dinosaur *Protoceratops* were found in Mongolia. Eggs were arranged in circles by the mother as they were laid in hollows in the sand. Hatchling fossils were also discovered. Judging by the number of nests, these dinosaurs, like *Maiasaura*, nested in colonies as do some birds today. *Maiasaura* went back to the same site year after year.

HOW BIG AN EGG?

● Dinosaur eggs are surprisingly small compared to the adults. The need for a shell thin enough to break on hatching sets a limit to the size of egg of land-living animals.

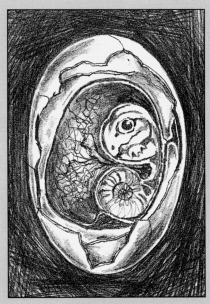

Protoceratops 6 ft (1.8 m) long

Which dinosaurs had horns?

The ceratopsians (horned-faces) were a group of dinosaurs common from 80 to 65 million years ago. Each kind had its own special pattern of horns and neck frill.

1 *Chasmosaurus*   **3** *Triceratops*   **5** *Torosaurus*
2 *Centrosaurus*   **4** *Styracosaurus*   **6** *Pentaceratops*

What were the horns for?

Horns could be used in defense, but, just as in deer and antelope today, they were probably used in fights between rival males too. Here two *Triceratops* are shown wrestling with locked horns. Horns may also have shown to rivals, or potential mates, an individual's strength.

As well as defense, the neck frill had an important everyday function. It was an attachment point for huge jaw muscles.

Triceratops

What did they fear?

With their powerful build, horns, and protective neck frill, a herd of ceratopsians such as *Centrosaurus* could drive off a meat-eater like *Tyrannosaurus*.

REPTILIAN RHINOS?

▽ A *Triceratops* skull head-on shows what powerful defenses it had. The animal weighed 5.5 tons but was built for running, with hoofs on the end of its toes. Behind the beak at the front of the jaw were powerful chopping teeth. The skull was 6.5 ft (2 m) long. *Torosaurus* had a skull 8 ft (2.4 m) long, the biggest of any land animal.

Triceratops 30 ft (9 m) long

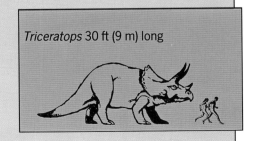

What used claws to kill?

Deinonychus and its relatives were meat-eaters that specialized in killing prey using a huge claw on each foot. They hunted in packs.

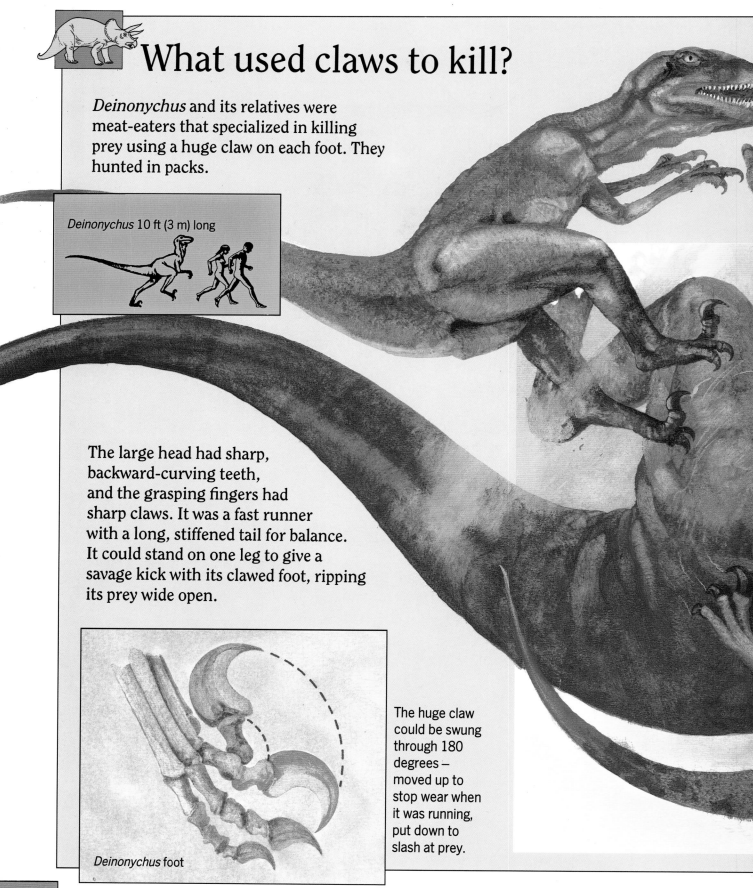

Deinonychus 10 ft (3 m) long

The large head had sharp, backward-curving teeth, and the grasping fingers had sharp claws. It was a fast runner with a long, stiffened tail for balance. It could stand on one leg to give a savage kick with its clawed foot, ripping its prey wide open.

Deinonychus foot

The huge claw could be swung through 180 degrees — moved up to stop wear when it was running, put down to slash at prey.

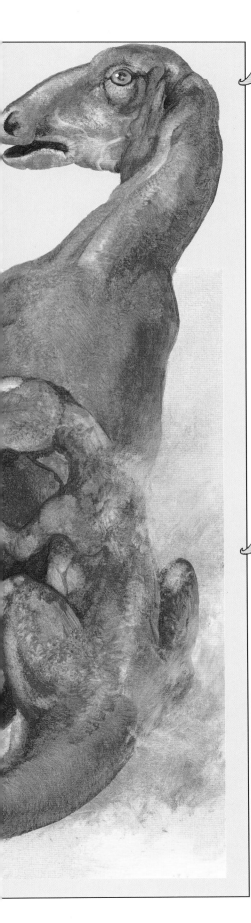

Fishing or hunting?

Baryonyx had a killing claw three times larger than those of *Deinonychus*, but not enough of its skeleton has been found to be sure it hunted in the same way. Its skull has the shape of a crocodile's, so some people think it fished with the aid of the huge claws on the hands (as shown below). Fish scales were found in the area of the fossil's stomach. But maybe the killing claws were on the feet?

Biggest killer of all?

Two gigantic fossil arms found in Mongolia, each 9 ft (2.6 m) long, are all that is known of the dinosaur to which they belonged. The three-fingered hands could rip open most animals. The shape of the arms suggests they belonged either to a giant ostrich dinosaur or, more terrifying still, to a huge version of *Deinonychus*.

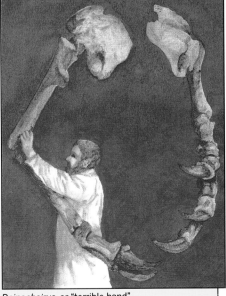

Deinocheirus, or "terrible-hand"

Who were the helmet heads?

About 80 million years ago, more than 25 species of dinosaur evolved that had crests on their heads. The crests looked like helmets. Males and females may have had crests of different colors. The crests acted as display signs showing what kind, and which sex, an individual was.

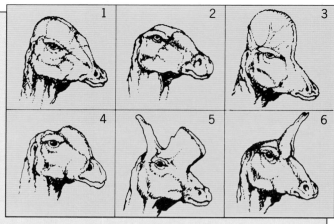

Six species of helmet-head dinosaurs

1 *Hypacrosaurus*	3 *Corythosaurus*	5 *Lambeosaurus*
2 *Edmontosaurus*	4 *Kritosaurus*	6 *Tsintaosaurus*

Did the duckbills fly?

Corythosaurus
33 ft (10 m) long

The helmet-head dinosaurs are also known as duckbills because they had flat snouts like a duck's bill. They were plant-eaters but they did not feed like ducks, fly or swim. They ate tough plant material – twigs, seeds and pine needles. At the side of their jaws they had plates of up to 2,000 massive grinding teeth.

Duckbills had long hind legs and the weight of the body in front was balanced by a long thick tail. They could stand upright on back legs alone to feed or look out for enemies, but generally they walked on all fours.

Did duckbills talk?

The crests of many duckbills were hollow, with air passages running through them. Some people thought that duckbills lived in water. They suggested the crests acted as snorkels or air stores for diving. But the snorkel had no hole at the tip, and the air store was too small to work. Now scientists think that duckbills spent most of their time on land and used the air tubes to make sounds. They may have worked like the tube on a trombone, to magnify sounds. People have made models of the crest tubes and blown down them. They make noises like horns. The different types of duckbill crest would have allowed each species to make a distinctive call as if talking to others of its kind. The air 75 to 65 million years ago may have been alive with the booming sounds of dinosaurs seeking a mate. *Parasaurolophus*, shown here, had the longest crest and probably the loudest voice.

An old idea was that *Parasaurolophus* used its crest as a snorkel

Parasaurolophus was 33 ft (10 m) long. Its crest was 6 ft (1.8 m) long.

Which dinosaurs wore crash helmets?

Towards the end of the Age of Dinosaurs one group of two-legged plant-eaters developed extraordinary thick skulls. These pachycephalosaurs (thick-headed reptiles) probably lived like sheep or goats today. The males took part in butting contests, and the thick skull served as a crash-helmet as their heads collided.

DID YOU KNOW...
● Most fossils of pachycephalosaurs are just pieces of skull roof — reflecting the strength and thickness of this bone compared to others in the body?
● The smallest thick-heads were little more than chicken sized?
● These dinosaurs had small teeth, which could be used for shredding plants?
● They had big eyes and a good sense of smell, and probably relied on these to give warning so they could avoid meat-eaters.

Pachycephalosaurus grew to 14.5 ft (4.5 m) or more. Most "thick-heads" were smaller.

BRAINS OR BONES?

Thick-headed dinosaurs did not have especially big brains. The dome of the skull was almost entirely bone, with extra knobs around the edges. Different types had different head shapes and arrangements of knobs, but all had strong domes. In some kinds, two different thicknesses (male and female?) are found in adults. Young ones had thinner heads.

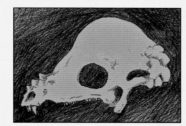

▽ *Pachycephalosaurus* had a 10 in- (25 cm-) thick bony skull roof.

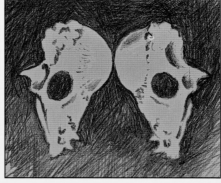

△ Skulls meet in the butting position.

BUILT FOR BUTTING?

● The joint between skull and backbone is different from most dinosaurs and would have allowed the domed part of the head to be thrust forward easily. Strong muscles and ligaments held the skull to the backbone.

● When heads clashed, spaces around the brain within the skull stopped it from being fatally jarred.

● The shock of impact was transmitted straight down the backbone, which was specially strengthened to absorb it. Each bone in the backbone had prongs to stop it from twisting against the next. There were more tough cords, turned to bone, wrapping the backbone and keeping it rigid.

● The hip bones were very firmly attached to the backbone, so a push from the back legs could be sent forward, or force from a knock on the head sent to the ground.

Which was like a tank?

Almost the size of a tank, and with the most complete armor-plating of all, *Ankylosaurus* and its close relatives had layers of bone over the skull, and big bony plates in the skin over the body, neck, tail, shoulders and thighs. A meat-eater had to try to turn one over to kill it.

Which dinosaurs had body armor?

As well as defending, these dinosaurs could attack. On the end of the tail was a club made of several bones joined into a solid mass. Strong muscles swung the tail to give a vicious blow. Even an attacking *Tyrannosaurus* could be knocked over or given a lethal blow with it.

As well as ankylosaurs there were nodosaurs, just as well armored, but without a tail club. There were also various spined and plated dinosaurs (see page 46). It was thought that the sauropod *Saltasaurus* was unusual because it had body armor, but recently more sauropod armored skin was found. More dinosaurs than we think may have had armor.

Ankylosaurus was 33 ft (10 m) long. It may have weighed 5.5 tons.

Saltasaurus (below) lived in Argentina 65 million years ago. Its armor (right) mixed small and large bony plates.

DID YOU KNOW...
● Ankylosaurs just lived late in the Age of Dinosaurs, but they make up nearly a tenth of all known dinosaurs? Is it just that their armor fossilized easily?
● With their weak jaws and small teeth, ankylosaurs probably ate soft plants? But some scientists think the smaller kinds fed on insects.

Were spines better than brains?

The spined dinosaurs were a group that lasted from 160 million years ago to, in some parts of the world, 65 million years ago. They were small-brained and moved slowly on all fours on elephant-like feet.

They do not seem to have developed special teeth for the plants they ate, yet still survived. The paired spines down their backs gave a defense that made up for their lack of advanced features.

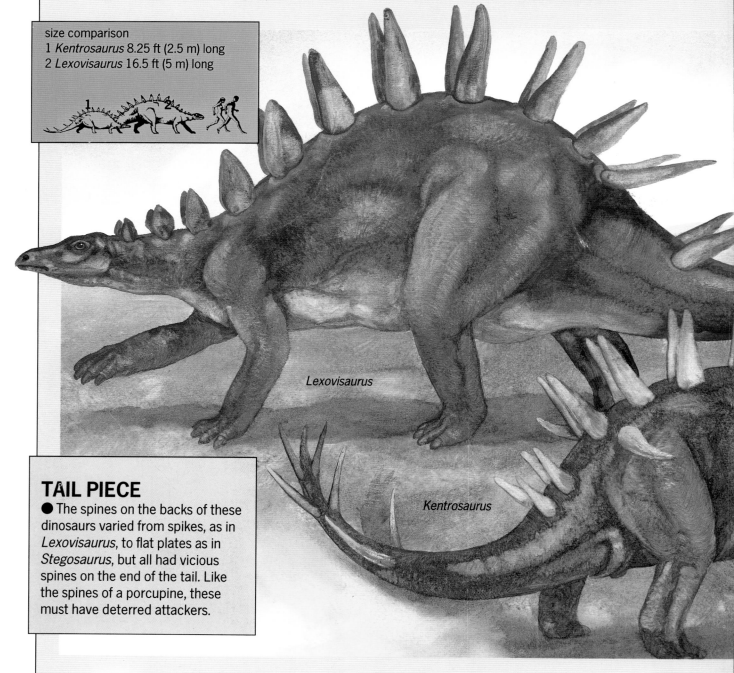

size comparison
1 *Kentrosaurus* 8.25 ft (2.5 m) long
2 *Lexovisaurus* 16.5 ft (5 m) long

Lexovisaurus

Kentrosaurus

TAIL PIECE
● The spines on the backs of these dinosaurs varied from spikes, as in *Lexovisaurus*, to flat plates as in *Stegosaurus*, but all had vicious spines on the end of the tail. Like the spines of a porcupine, these must have deterred attackers.

Stegosaurus 24.75 ft (7.5 m) long, the largest of the spined dinosaurs.

A *Stegosaurus* fights off an *Allosaurus*.

WORLDWIDE SUCCESS?

● Spined dinosaurs have been found in North America, Europe, China, India and Africa.

● *Scelidosaurus* (below) lived 185 million years ago. Its remains were found in England. It was 13 ft (4 m) long overall, and its skin was studded with bones, including low spines. It may have been the ancestor of spined dinosaurs.

● *Lexovisaurus* lived about 160 million years ago in France and England. *Kentrosaurus*, from 145 million years ago, was found in Tanzania.

● The spines at the end of *Stegosaurus'* tail were each nearly 3.3 ft (1 m) long.

● *Stegosaurus* was tallest at the hips. Its head was small and low.

INDEX